# Contents

# Foreword

It is five years since *Harry Potter and the Philosopher's Stone* was first published. Since then millions of copies of J.K. Rowling's four books about Harry have sold throughout the world. They are available in 47 different languages, from Albanian to Zulu. They continue to occupy the bestseller lists. Sales climb and climb. The fifth book, apparently entitled *Harry Potter and the Order of the Phoenix*, is eagerly awaited by readers of all ages.

This is a story even J.K. Rowling couldn't have imagined. Each chapter becomes more extraordinary, more statistically mind-blowing. The film of the first book, released in the autumn of 2001, broke all box office records. First editions of the books – if they haven't been read to a pulp – are reputed to fetch extraordinary sums at auction. Harry Potter merchandising dominates toyshops worldwide, some of it already earmarked as collectors' items.

And it all began during a train journey.

Some of us remember reading *Harry Potter and the Philosopher's Stone* knowing nothing about the book, its author, the characters or even that there would be sequels. Who now doesn't know that Harry Potter is a wizard?

J.K. Rowling gives very few interviews. When she does she emphasizes that, apart from the publishing sensation of which she is the creator, she isn't very different from many of the rest of us. No news tends to mean that some journalists make it up (Rita Skeeter was no idle invention). Stories abound about the future of the series and the author's personal life. In this conversation, she had absolutely no doubt that she would complete the seven books she originally envisaged. Those who know her are no less confident but believe that she will do it in her own good time.

Towards the end of the conversation, which took place before the launch of the epic *Harry Potter and the Goblet of Fire*, J.K. Rowling reflected with some regret on the pressures of fame. They were nothing compared to what she faces today – demands on her time, her money, her patronage – over and above the business of writing. The industry that grew from that moment on a train is all down to one woman – J.K. Rowling. It's a colossal responsibility for one human being.

The world of books for young people now basks in a previously unknown golden glow of attention and recognition. J.K. Rowling's novels, together with those of several other writers, have undoubtedly changed that literary landscape forever. Sometimes it seems that those very books are in danger of being submerged under the hype that accompanies their every move. But nothing can detract from the way in which children have taken them to their hearts and imaginations. At the core of the industry with all its trademarks, soft toys, key rings and beach balls sit those old-fashioned, totally reliable bound bundles of paper and print – the Harry Potter books.

Lindsey Fraser

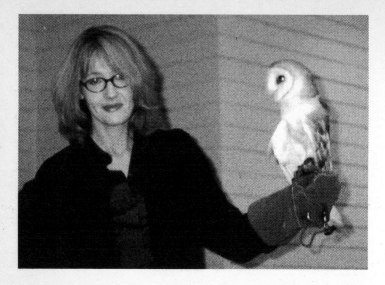

*J.K. Rowling is the author of the phenomenally popular series of books about the child wizard Harry Potter. The success in 1997 of her first-ever published book,* Harry Potter and the Philosopher's Stone, *catapulted her to world fame, and has been made into a film by Warner Bros. The four books published so far in this seven-book series have won worldwide critical acclaim for their author, including The Smarties Gold Award, the Whitbread Children's Book of the Year Award, the British Book Awards Children's Book of the Year, the Prix Sorcière, the Scottish Arts Council Children's Book Award, the American Booksellers Book of the Year Award, and many more.*

An interview with
# J.K. Rowling
*by Lindsey Fraser*


# My family and my childhood

## Where did you come in the family?

I was the older of two girls. My earliest memory is of my sister being born – she's just under two years younger than me. My dad gave me playdough the day she arrived, to keep me occupied while he ran in and out of the bedroom. I have no memory of seeing the new baby, but I do remember eating the playdough.

## Were books important in your family?

Another early memory is of having the measles – I must

have been about four – and Dad reading *The Wind in the Willows*. I don't remember feeling ill at all – just lying there listening to those stories. Both my parents loved reading. My mother was a huge reader – she was quite bookish – and never happier than when she was curled up, reading. That was a big influence on me. She came from a family of teachers and I think my dad followed her example.

## Tell us about your grandparents.

My grandfathers were called Ernie and Stanley – I named the driver and conductor of the Knight Bus which comes to rescue Harry Potter after them. They were both great characters. Ernie owned a supermarket, and when we went to stay – they lived in a flat above the shop – he would let my sister and me play shops after hours with real tins and packets and money. Just as long as we put everything back.

Stanley sometimes had a problem telling fact from fiction. He was a great dreamer, and spent a lot of time in his garden shed, making things.

One of my grandmothers was called Kathleen – my middle name. I adored her, and my saddest memory of that time is of her death. My other grandmother was obsessed with dogs, which she much preferred to humans. There was a touch of Aunt Marge in her, to tell the truth.

## Did you have any pets?

When I was very, very tiny we had a dog called Thumper, named after the rabbit in the Disney film, *Bambi*. I was very sad when he was put down. We had two guinea pigs later on, but they were eaten by a fox. I remember the scene of carnage on the back lawn – it was *not* pleasant . . . And we had another dog, Misty, who was around until after I went to university.

As a teenager I had tropical fish. That was a big hobby and I still love them.

## Where were you born?

In Chipping Sodbury, near Bristol. I'm very proud of that! I think it probably doomed me to a love of weird place-names. Until I was about nine we lived in and around Bristol, and then we moved to Tutshill, a little village near Chepstow in South Wales. It is a town dominated by a castle on a cliff, which might explain a lot.

## Why did you move to the country?

I think it was really a dream of my parents', both of whom had urban childhoods. They met on a train heading north to Scotland from King's Cross Station in London. Dad was in the navy and Mum was a Wren, and they were both travelling to a posting in Arbroath, just north of Dundee. It was love at first sight; they married at 19 and had me at 20. They both dreamed of life in a country cottage, and my dad could commute easily from Chepstow to his work at the Rolls Royce factory.

## Tell us about the place where you lived.

Our house was a cottage next to the church. It had

originally been the village school. All our friends thought it was spooky living next to a graveyard but we liked it. I still love graveyards – they are a great source of names. We lived near Offa's Dyke on the River Wye – a wonderful place. We used to love exploring amongst the boulders.

When we got older, of course, it became boring. There wasn't as much to interest teenagers.

## What else do you remember from that time?

One of my happiest memories is of a family holiday in Norfolk. I am very close to my sister now, but when we were younger we fought like cat and dog. For some reason we were getting on unnaturally well during that holiday, and I just remember all the late-night laughing, the stories and jokes. I think my parents were surprised but relieved.

\*   \*   \*

# My schooldays

## What do you remember about your time at school?

My first school was on the outskirts of Bristol and I absolutely loved it, although I remember on my first day, when Mum came to pick me up for lunch, I thought that was it and that I'd 'done' school and wouldn't need to go back.

The village school in Tutshill was pretty Dickensian – a complete contrast to the open-plan school I was used to. We were seated according to the teacher's perception of our brightness, and after ten minutes she put me in the 'dim' row. There are a number of people who influenced the character of Snape in my books, and that teacher was definitely one of them. I found it extremely scary. We used to have The Daily Ten – mental arithmetic – and on my first day I got half a point. Well, I'd never done fractions before! I think that I grew on that teacher in time, but I remember having to work hard at it. And at the fractions.

## What was your secondary school like?

I quite liked secondary school, but I was particularly influenced by my English teacher, Miss Shepherd. She was strict, and could be quite caustic, but she was very conscientious. I really respected her because she was a teacher who was passionate about teaching us. She was an introduction to a different kind of woman, I suppose. She was a feminist, and clever. She had this incredibly no-nonsense approach. I remember doodling while she was talking one day and she told me that I was being very rude indeed. I said, 'But I'm listening,' and she told me that I was still being rude. That really stuck with me. She never just said, 'Don't do that.' Her approach made far more of an impression. So I loved English. Miss Shepherd was very hot on structure and refused to allow us to be the least bit sloppy. Even though I read a great deal, it was very good to be shown exactly what gave writing structure and pace. I learned such a lot from her and we're still in touch. She was the only teacher I ever confided in. She inspired trust.

When *Harry Potter and the Philosopher's Stone* was published she sent me a letter via Bloomsbury, the publisher. Her comments meant more to me than any newspaper review, because I knew she would never have written anything unless she meant it. She was the personification of integrity. *And* she liked the book.

When I was in the Upper Sixth a very important thing happened. A boy called Sean Harris came to school, having been at school in Cyprus – his dad was in the army. He became my best friend – *Harry Potter and the Chamber of Secrets* is dedicated to him.

He had a turquoise Ford Anglia which spelled freedom for me. When you live in a village in the country, driving is very important. So you can imagine that I couldn't have just any old car rescuing Harry and Ron Weasley to take them to Hogwarts – it *had* to be a turquoise Ford Anglia. Ron Weasley isn't a living portrait of Sean, but he really is very Sean-ish.

It often isn't until I re-read what I've written that I realise where certain bits of my stories have come from. Harry was rescued by that car, just as the car rescued me from my boredom. It's one of the very few bits I can think of that have such a direct connection with real life. That, and when Harry looks in the mirror and sees his family waving to him. That was a very important image from my life, when I lost my mother.

## Did you like all your teachers?

No, not all of them. My least favourite teacher was just a bully. I've met quite a few teachers now, both when I was teaching and when I've been visiting schools, and the bullies really do stand out. I understand from the teacher's point of view that it's very easy to be a bully, but it's also the worst, shabbiest thing you can do. We're back to Snape here.

## Was there anything else you didn't like?

My least favourite subject was metalwork. I was the worst in my class – just terrible. I am *not* a practical person . . . It seemed to me to be all about hammering stuff until I broke it. I did try, but I just could not do it.

Mum always kept a ridiculous flat teaspoon I made which was useless, completely hopeless. I was terrible at woodwork too – I remember arriving home with a photograph frame composed mainly of glue.

I was also dreadful at sport, although I vaguely liked gym. I especially hated hockey. But I did like swimming and dancing.

And I *loathed* the uniform. It was brown and yellow, two colours I will now never, ever wear on principle.

## Do you think your teachers thought you would become a writer?

I think Miss Shepherd might have believed I could be a writer but I don't think she expected it of me. I always, always wanted to be a writer but I *never* shared my burning ambition with anyone.

When I was about six I wrote a book – just a little story – and when I finished it I remember thinking, well now we can publish this. I wanted the complete experience, even then. I was a lot less arrogant by the time I was 26. By then, I didn't think I had any chance whatsoever.

## Can you describe what you were like as a child?

I think I was always very insecure, a real worrier, but I would put on a show of confidence to mask it. By 11 or 12, I *might* just have been a tiny bit Hermione-ish. I always felt I had to achieve, my hand always had to be the first to go up, I always had to be right. Maybe it was because I felt quite plain in comparison to my sister. I probably felt I had to compensate.

I did relax as I got older which was a good thing, although I was still – and am still – a worrier. I was very lucky in having such good friends. That was especially important in my teens, when my mother became ill with multiple sclerosis. Anyone who has experienced something like this happening in their family will know the huge knock-on effect, and the stress involved. Friends become even more important, to talk to, to confide in.

## What did you read?

I remember reading lots of *Noddy* with Mum. She was a great Enid Blyton fan. I'm not. I did read the *Famous Five* books, or at least some of them, but not much else.

I absolutely loved the Richard Scarry books. That first book I wrote aged six was a complete rip-off. I've kept some of those books from my childhood and my daughter loves them too.

I was completely horse-obsessed and had a picture book version of Anna Sewell's *Black Beauty* when I was about eight. I'd cry my eyes out at that story. I also read *Little Women* by Louisa May Alcott when I was eight, and that began my '*Little Women* Phase'. I *was* Jo March for a few months.

But my favourite book was *The Little White Horse* by Elizabeth Goudge. It was probably something to do with the fact that the heroine was quite plain, but it is a very well-constructed and clever book, and the more you read it, the cleverer it appears. And perhaps more than any other book, it has a direct influence on the Harry Potter books. The author always included details of what her characters were eating and I remember liking that. You may have noticed that I always list the food being eaten at Hogwarts.

The important thing is that no book was ever forbidden or censored, except once, when, as a present, I'd been given a spin-off book from the TV programme *The New Avengers*. It had a very violent beginning which disturbed me, and I was glad when Mum said – it was the only time she did – that I shouldn't read any more. Other than that we read *anything*. I read Jane Austen's *Pride and Prejudice* when I was 11 or 12 and *Vanity Fair* by W.M. Thackeray when I was 14. I know that sounds precocious but it was there, so I read it.

I was like my mother – I'd read anything and everything. Even now, if I visit a strange bathroom in which someone has been inconsiderate enough not to have provided books to read, I'll read the labels on the toiletries.

I had an aunt who was a reader for the publishers Mills and Boon – she read manuscripts – and she would pass on those books too, so I'd read all these romantic novels in about one hour flat. I remember when I was nine reading my first James Bond novel – Ian Fleming's *Thunderball* – and being fascinated by the Bloody Marys they drank. There was something wonderful about a drink with tomato juice in it. I love Bloody Marys now . . .

We were very, very lucky – we were bought lots of books.

## Did you read poetry?

I must admit to having a slight blind spot about poetry. I enjoyed the children's treasuries we had, but I don't think it could have been a great love of my mother's – and poetry isn't something I reach for now.

## What do you enjoy reading now?

I love novels and biographies. I've got a bit of an obsession about the Kennedys – President John F. Kennedy's family. I started one of my book tours to America in Boston, and insisted on making a detour to visit the Kennedy Museum there. I was going on and on about the family to my driver until, just before we arrived, she told me that she'd dated Teddy Kennedy. The things she could have told me if I'd only given her the chance . . .

My most influential writer, without a doubt, is Jessica Mitford. When my great aunt gave me *Hons and Rebels* when I was 14 she instantly became my heroine. She ran away from home to fight in the civil war in Spain, taking with her a camera that she had charged to her father's account. I wished I'd had the nerve to do something like that. She had tremendous moral courage and did some physically brave things as a human rights activist. I love her sense of humour, her great independence. She stood up against her family – they were very rich indeed and didn't believe in educating girls – and showed her passion by acting on what she believed, not preaching. I love the way she never outgrew some of her adolescent traits, remaining true to her politics – she was a self-taught socialist – throughout her life. I think I've read everything she wrote. I even called my daughter after her.

# What kinds of music do you like?

I like all sorts of music, and I still listen to music I liked when I was 17. Neither of my parents was interested in classical music – they loved The Beatles and other 60s stuff, and I like those too. I played the acoustic guitar and would fantasise about playing an electric guitar solo. I still like The Beatles. My favourite group in all the world is The Smiths. And when I was going through a punky phase, it was The Clash.

# Do you enjoy art?

I loved art at school and I still draw for pleasure. For some reason – maybe it was because I knew I would never make a living out of it – I never minded showing people my drawings and paintings. I *never* show my writing to anybody. My editor will tell you! I find it so hard to let go. It's too important. I hate it when people ask to see my rough drafts – they're too personal, somehow.

I love art galleries. I've now been to New York on book tours several times – it's one of my favourite places – and I've yet to visit any of the fabulous galleries there. I'm always desperate to go but there's never an afternoon free.

In my early 20s, I had a passion for Gainsborough, especially a painting called *The Morning Walk*. It is of the most extraordinary couple – the man is very striking while the woman is quite wishy-washy – and the explanation was that this painting was done for their marriage. I wondered how that marriage worked out and something told me it hadn't.

Perhaps my favourite painting is Caravaggio's *Supper at Emmaus* when Jesus reveals himself to the disciples having risen from the dead. I love it. Jesus looks very likeable – soft and rounded – and the painting captures the exact moment when the disciples realise who this man is, blessing their bread.

## Did you go to the theatre or the cinema?

We went to pantomimes in London. I remember in one production of *Peter Pan* we were asked to hiss at Captain

Hook, and Dad booed. Captain Hook came off the stage and all the way up to our seats – I was terrified.

I love going to the theatre now. The first play I saw was at Stratford-upon-Avon. It was a sixth form outing and we saw Shakespeare's *King Lear*. I was absolutely electrified by it. We also saw *The Winter's Tale* and that was where I found the name Hermione – although of course it didn't come in handy until years later.

I like the cinema. There was no cinema in Chepstow so we didn't go much when I was a child. My favourite film then was *The Jungle Book*. I also liked the film of Richard Adams' *Watership Down* – of course, it's a wonderful book.

I think my favourite film star would probably be Michael Caine, although I had a massive crush on Dustin Hoffman after I saw him in *Little Big Man*. I've still got a bit of a thing about him . . .

## Did you watch much television as a child?

Not really. My parents wouldn't have the TV on much.

I loved cartoons – I still do – especially *Wacky Races*. And I loved *The Monkees* – in fact I was in love with Davy Jones. When my daughter was very small I would ask her to call me when *Animaniacs* started on a Saturday morning, and she would come and bounce up and down on my bed to wake me up.

Recently, because I've been writing so much and away a lot, I've hardly watched television. Sometimes I've even missed important things on the news. I try never to miss *The Royle Family* though – that is a brilliant series.

\*     \*     \*

# My career

## What did you do when you left school?

I went to Exeter University for four years, including a year teaching English in Paris which I loved. At first Exeter was a bit of a shock. I was expecting to be amongst lots of similar people – thinking radical thoughts. But it wasn't like that. However, once I'd made friends with some like-minded people I began to enjoy myself. Although I don't think I worked as hard as I could have.

## Why did you choose to study languages when you loved English literature so much?

That was a bit of a mistake. I certainly didn't do *everything* my parents told me, but I think I was influenced by their belief that languages would be better for finding a job. I don't regret it hugely, but it was a strange decision for someone who only really wanted to be a writer, not that I'd had the courage to tell anyone that, of course.

## Where did you go once you had graduated?

That was an even bigger mistake. I went to London to do a bilingual secretarial course (a course for secretaries who can speak more than one language). I was – am – totally unsuited to that kind of work. Me as a secretary? I'd be your worst nightmare.

But the one thing I did learn to do was to type. Now I type all my own books, so that's been incredibly useful. I'm pretty fast.

When I finished the course I just wanted to find a job – any job – that would earn a living to give me time to write. In fact, I landed a job with Amnesty International as a research assistant into human rights abuses in Francophone Africa (the part of Africa where people mainly speak French). It meant that I was working with representatives of over 100 nationalities – all under the one roof. That made it a very, very interesting place to work, and worthwhile. If I wasn't writing full-time it was important that my time was being spent on something worthwhile.

I'm not sure that many of the people working there at the time would remember me, because at lunch-times, when they were all off to the pub, I would make some kind of excuse and rush off to a café or another pub to write. I was working on an adult novel. I was sharing a flat at the time, and again, to get away, I would head for the local cafés. They were the ideal place to go and write – especially for someone who wasn't being honest about what she was up to. So that's how my passion for writing in cafés started.

## When did the idea for Harry Potter first enter your head?

My boyfriend was moving to Manchester and wanted me to move too. It was during the train journey back from Manchester to London, after a weekend looking for a flat, that Harry Potter made his appearance. I have never felt such a huge rush of excitement. I knew *immediately* that this was going to be such fun to write.

I didn't know then that it was going to be a book for children – I just knew that I had this boy, Harry. During that journey I also discovered Ron, Nearly Headless Nick, Hagrid and Peeves. But with the idea of my life careering round my head, I didn't have a pen that worked! And I never went *anywhere* without my pen and notebook. So rather than trying to write it, I had to think it. And I think that was a very good thing. I was besieged by a mass of detail, and if it didn't survive that journey, it probably wasn't worth remembering.

Hogwarts School of Witchcraft and Wizardry was the first thing I concentrated on. I was thinking of a place of great order, but immense danger, with children who had skills with which they could overwhelm their teachers. Logically it had to be set in a secluded place, and pretty soon I settled on Scotland in my mind. I think it was in subconscious tribute to where my parents had married. People keep saying they know what I based Hogwarts on – but they're all wrong. I have never seen a castle anywhere that looks the way I imagine Hogwarts.

So I got back to the flat that night and began to write it all down in a tiny cheap notebook. I wrote lists of all the subjects to be studied – I knew there had to be seven. The characters came first, and then I had to find names to fit them. Gilderoy Lockhart is a good example. I knew his name had to have an impressive ring to it. I was looking through the *Dictionary of Phrase and Fable* – a great source for names – and came across Gilderoy, a handsome Scottish highwayman. Exactly what I wanted. And then I found Lockhart on a war memorial to the First World War. The two together said everything I wanted about the character.

## Can you describe the process of creating the stories?

It was a question of discovering why Harry was where he was, why his parents were dead. I was inventing it, but it felt like research. By the end of that train journey I knew it was going to be a seven book series. I know that's extraordinarily arrogant for somebody who had never been published, but that's how it came to me. It took me five years to plan the series out, to plot through each of the seven novels. I know what and who's coming when, and it can feel like greeting old friends. Professor Lupin, who appears in the third book, is one of my favourite characters. He's a damaged person, literally and metaphorically. I think it's important for children to know that adults, too, have their problems, that they struggle. His being a werewolf is really a metaphor for people's reactions to illness and disability.

I almost always have complete histories for my characters. If I put all that detail in, each book would be the size of the *Encyclopaedia Britannica*, but I do have to be careful that I don't just assume that the reader knows as much as I do. Sirius Black is a good example. I have a whole childhood worked out for him. The readers don't need to know that but I do. I need to know much more than them because I'm the one moving the characters across the page.

I invented the game of Quidditch after a huge row with the boyfriend I lived with in Manchester. I stormed out of the house, went to the pub – and invented Quidditch.

## Did you give up work to write the books?

Oh no! I moved to Manchester and worked for the Manchester Chamber of Commerce – rather briefly, because almost immediately I was made redundant. I then went to work at the University but I was really very unhappy. My mother had died about a month after I moved there. And then we were burgled, and everything my mother had left me was stolen. People were incredibly kind and friendly, but I decided that I wanted to get away.

I knew that I'd enjoyed teaching English as a foreign language in Paris and I thought to myself, how would it be if I went abroad, did some teaching, took my manuscript, had some sun . . . ? That's how I came to live in Oporto in Portugal, teaching students aged eight to sixty-two. They were mostly teenagers preparing for exams, but there were also business people and housewives. The teenagers aged between 14 and 17 years were easily my favourite. They were so full of ideas and possibilities, forming opinions. I became head of that department.

After six months, I met my husband-to-be, a journalist. We married, and the next year had Jessica — just before my 28th birthday. That was, without doubt, the best moment of my life. At that point, I had completed the first three chapters of *Harry Potter and the Philosopher's Stone*, almost exactly as they appear in the published book. The rest of the book was in rough draft.

## Why did you move to Edinburgh?

It became clear that my marriage wasn't working, and I decided that it would be easier if I came back to Britain. My job wasn't tremendously secure, and of course it stopped completely over the summer holidays. I was worried about finding work during that period, especially with a small baby. I came to Edinburgh to stay with my sister for Christmas, and I thought, I can be happy here. And I have been.

The only people I knew in Edinburgh were my sister and her best friend. I'd only met my sister's husband once before. Most of my friends were in London, but I felt that Edinburgh was the kind of city in which I wanted to bring up my child. Pretty soon I made some good friends. Maybe it was my Scottish blood calling me home.

## How did you continue to write?

I decided to return to teaching to earn a living, but first I had to get the qualification – a Post-Graduate Certificate in Education. That would take a year, so I knew that unless I made a push to finish the first book now, I might never finish it. I made a huge, superhuman effort. I would put Jessica in her pushchair, take her to the park and try to tire her out. When she fell asleep I'd rush to a café and write. Not all the cafés I went to approved of me sitting there for a couple of hours having bought only one cup of coffee . . . But my brother-in-law had just opened his own café – Nicolson's – and I thought they might be welcoming. I was careful to go when they weren't busy, and the staff were very nice. I used to joke about what I'd do for them if I ever got published and the book sold well . . . I still wasn't sure that I'd ever be published. So my first book was finished in Nicolson's.

I typed the manuscript out on a manual typewriter. I'd read in the *Writers' and Artists' Year Book* that the optimum length for a children's novel was 40,000 words – mine was 90,000! To try to disguise this, I typed it in single-line spacing (with the lines close together), but I didn't fool anybody. I had to type it all out again, double-line spaced (with the lines further apart). I'd sneak into the Open Access computers in college at weekends, or type with Jessica at my feet working her way through piles of jigsaws. I was terrified that people would discover that I wasn't doing my course work.

The first agent I sent the manuscript to returned it. The first publisher I sent the manuscript to returned it. So I sent it off again. The second agent, Christopher Little, took it on – his letter is one of the best I've ever received. It took a year to find a publisher but when

Bloomsbury accepted it, it was definitely the second-best moment in my life – after Jessica.

A year later, July 1997, the book was published – I walked around all day with a finished copy tucked under my arm. The first time I saw it in a bookshop I had this mad desire to sign it. It was an extraordinary moment. The first two words Jessica could read were 'Harry' and 'Potter', and she'd yell them out in bookshops. I was sure people would think I was making her do it . . .

## What happened after 'Harry Potter and the Philosopher's Stone' was published?

My publisher was very encouraging and told me it was selling surprisingly well. There was no great fanfare – a good review in *The Scotsman*, followed by some others – but mostly it seems to have been word of mouth. Then my American publisher, Scholastic, bought the rights to the first book for more money than anyone had expected. The burst of publicity terrified me. I was teaching part-time by then, and trying to write *Harry Potter and the Chamber of Secrets*. I felt frozen by all the attention.

## What made you decide to become a full-time writer?

It wasn't an easy decision. I didn't know whether this was all just a flash in the pan. And I had my daughter to think of. But I thought that I could probably afford to write full-time for two years, although I was risking my teaching career because I wouldn't gain the experience necessary to go back to it as a career. When I won the Smarties Book Prize, sales started to climb. I got my first royalty cheque. I didn't expect to earn any royalties – not for a first novel – so that was a very proud moment.

It wasn't a great start, though, because I found *Harry Potter and the Chamber of Secrets* incredibly hard to finish. I was worried that it wouldn't live up to readers' expectations – I'd heard that your second novel is the hardest to write. In the end I delivered the manuscript on time but took it back for six weeks until I was satisfied with it.

## Did you receive many letters from your readers?

I remember my first ever fan letter, from Francesca Gray. It began, 'Dear Sir . . . ' I've since met her. There was a growing trickle of mail, but when the book began to sell well in America the letters poured in. I realised that I was fast becoming my own inefficient secretary. It was a really nice problem to have, but it was time to hire someone to do things properly.

## What happened when 'Harry Potter and the Chamber of Secrets' was published?

It went almost straight to number one in the bestseller lists, which I thought was incredible. You have to remember that these things were taking me hugely by surprise. The fact is that it all happened very quickly but what mattered was that I had written a book I was proud of.

## And 'Harry Potter and the Prisoner of Azkaban'?

The idea that children would queue up in bookshops to buy copies of my books delighted me. But there are other more disconcerting sides to that level of publicity – having your photograph appear regularly in the papers is not something I ever anticipated.

But all the time, children are reading the books. And we know now that adults are reading the books, too. And they like them. That's what I remember when I'm feeling besieged.

## Did the publicity quieten down?

No! I thought it must have reached saturation point – surely – but the announcement that the film rights for the first book had been bought by Warner Bros. increased press interest.

# Are you happy about Harry Potter being made into a film?

I am now. We were inundated with offers from film companies, and I said no to all of them – even Warner. But they kept coming back. I'm not against the idea of a film – I love films. The vital thing for me was that it would be true to the book, and I have great faith in Warner's commitment to that. Obviously there are some things that won't 'work' on screen, but I didn't want the plot to change very much at all. The decision to go with Warner wasn't about money or power, it was because I believed in them. I'd also seen their screen adaptations of *The Secret Garden* and *The Little Princess*, and I thought they were very good.

They've given me a lot of input, sent me maps and drawings of Hogwarts to make sure that when it appears on film it will be close to my vision of the place. The crucial thing is that the characters won't be led off in any inappropriate directions.

The thing I'm most looking forward to is seeing Quidditch. I've been watching it in my head for nine years now – and finally I'll get to see it along with everybody else.

## Did your editor at Scholastic make many changes for the American edition?

Not very many at all. I read somewhere that the books had been 'translated into American' and that's just nonsense. Changes were only made when words meant something completely different in America. A good example is 'jumper'. If I'd left that as it is in the British edition, Harry, Ron and Fred would all have been wearing pinafore dresses as far as the American readers are concerned, and I was more than happy to substitute 'sweater' to avoid that confusion! All Hagrid's dialect was left intact. The changes really were minimal.

The only thing I was uncomfortable about was that an American copy editor changed all the 'mums' to 'moms', and I just wasn't happy with that. Mrs Weasley is *not* a 'mom'. So that's been reversed and they've been kept as 'mums' for the other books.

## What happened when you went to promote 'Harry Potter and the Prisoner of Azkaban' in America?

On my previous tour, the greatest number of people at an event was probably about 100. My second tour began in Boston. As we were driving up to the bookshop I saw a massive queue snaking along two blocks. I asked Kris, from the publisher, Scholastic, if there was a sale on and she told me the queue was for me. It was the most extraordinary experience. They whisked me in the back entrance and took me upstairs, and when I walked through the door there was all this screaming and lots of flash bulbs going off. It was the nearest I'll ever come to being a pop star. I was totally speechless; I didn't know what to do with my face. I wanted to look friendly but I have a feeling I looked guilty and shifty. I signed one thousand four hundred books that day.

## Do you enjoy the book tours?

The thing I enjoy best – apart from writing the books –

is meeting the readers. Answering their questions is pure pleasure. This world that I've had in my head for years is now out there and in other peoples' heads! I love it. There are readers all over the world who are now intimate with characters that only I knew about until three years ago.

## Your books have now been translated into at least 28 languages. What do you think of the different versions?

I've recently received copies of the first *Harry* translated into Japanese – it's beautiful. But I think the one I'm most impressed with is the Greek translation.

Sometimes I find strange little aberrations. In the Spanish translation Neville Longbottom's toad – which he's always losing – has been translated as a turtle. Which surely makes losing it rather more difficult. And there's no mention of water for it to live in. I don't want to think too much about that . . . In the Italian translation, Professor Dumbledore has been translated into Professore Silencio. The translator has taken the 'dumb' from the name and based the translation on that. In fact 'dumbledore' is the old English word for bumblebee. I chose it because my image is of this benign wizard, always on the move, humming to himself, and I loved the sound of the word too. For me 'Silencio' is a complete contradiction. But the book is very popular in Italy – so it obviously doesn't bother the Italians!

## Do you think you'll finish all seven Harry Potter novels?

Absolutely – if only for myself.

## What will you do once you've finished the seventh?

It will be the most incredible thing to finish the books. It will have been a very long time to spend with those characters in my head and I know I'll be sad to leave them. But I know I *will* leave them alone.

I'm sure I'll always write, at least until I lose my marbles. I'm very, very lucky. Because of Harry's success, I don't need to do it financially, nobody's making me. I just need to do it for myself. Sometimes I think I'm temperamentally suited to being a moderately successful writer, with the focus of attention on the books rather than on me. It was wonderful enough just to be published. The greatest reward is the enthusiasm of the readers.

There are times – and I don't want to sound ungrateful – when I would gladly give back some of the money in exchange for time and peace to write. That's been the greatest strain, especially during the writing of the fourth book. I've become famous, and I'm not very comfortable with that. Because of the fame some really difficult things have happened, and it's required a great effort of will to shut them out. And I've also had to juggle the pressure to promote each book with the pressure from readers – and myself – to finish the next one. There have been some black weeks when I've wondered whether it's worth it. But I've ploughed on, and book four is exactly what I want it to be.

If you look at any famous person, there are always

problems attached and they're not pleasant. But I still know that I'm an extraordinarily lucky person, doing what I love best in all the world.

May 2000

# J.K. Rowling's Books

## An overview by Lindsey Fraser

Muggles, Dementors, Quidditch, Knuts, the Whomping Willow – if these words sound alien to you, then you have yet to be introduced to the world of Harry Potter and his friends. And his enemies.

Since *Harry Potter and the Philosopher's Stone* was published in 1997, the world that J.K. Rowling first imagined during a train journey from Manchester to London one Sunday evening has become familiar to millions of people throughout the world. The stunning and rapid success of her books is unprecedented, drawing readers into two co-existing worlds – the ordinary Muggle world of humans and the extraordinary world of magic.

## But just who is Harry Potter?

J.K. Rowling has always insisted that there will be seven Harry Potter novels and with the publication of *Harry Potter and the Goblet of Fire* we are now over half way through his career at Hogwarts. But it is still true to say that nobody, with the exception of the author, knows exactly who Harry Potter is.

We do know various things about him. We know that he is an orphan, that he survived the murderous intentions of the evil wizard Voldemort, and that he did not know, until he was 11 years old, that he was a wizard. There were a few indications that Harry was no ordinary boy. For example, his hair grew long overnight, not quite covering the mysterious lightning-shaped scar on his forehead, defying even the most brutal of haircuts. And there was the time, during a visit to the zoo, that a conversation with a Brazilian boa constrictor resulted in the snake gliding to freedom hissing, 'Brazil, here I come . . . Thanksss, amigo.' Nobody was more surprised by this than Harry, and he was instantly blamed for it. As far as his Uncle Vernon is concerned, everything that isn't normal is Harry's fault, and Uncle Vernon hates anything that isn't completely normal.

The opening of the first novel about Harry, *Harry Potter and the Philosopher's Stone*, makes that aversion to anything out of the ordinary absolutely clear.

> *Mr and Mrs Dursley, of number four Privet Drive, were proud to say that they were perfectly normal, thank you very much. They were the last people you'd expect to be involved in anything strange or mysterious, because they just didn't hold with such nonsense.*

Vernon and Petunia Dursley were forced to look after their nephew when he was abandoned on their doorstep as a baby, accompanied by a letter which presumably explained his tragic circumstances. They were horrified by the discovery and made Harry live in the cupboard under the stairs, treating him appallingly, in contrast to the overwhelming, blind devotion they showed to their odious son, Dudley.

For his first 11 years, Harry had no idea whatsoever that he was special. His aunt and uncle told him that his parents had died in a car crash. They were unfailingly unpleasant to him, and went out of their way to exclude him from treats or family events.

The truth is that Vernon and Petunia Dursley were terrified of Harry. They knew in their heart of hearts that he must be powerful, and that scared them. Even before he came to live with them they tried desperately to avoid facing the truth about Mrs Dursley's family. Mr Dursley's reaction to a conversation he overhears about the Potters and their son, Harry, shows that the problem is rarely far from his mind.

*Mr Dursley stopped dead. Fear flooded him. He looked back at the whisperers as if he wanted to say something to them, but thought better of it.*

*He dashed back across the road, hurried up to his office, snapped at his secretary not to disturb him, seized his telephone and had almost finished dialling his home number when he changed his mind. He put the receiver down and stroked his moustache, thinking . . . no, he was being stupid. Potter wasn't such an unusual name. He was sure there were lots of people called Potter who had a son called Harry.*

Once Harry has come to live with them, the need to disguise the truth increases. But with every day that passes they know that the time will come when he must discover his true identity – or at least some clues towards it. Although it is impossible not to despise the Dursleys, it's important to remember how frightened they must have been. So frightened that they could never discuss the situation sensibly with each other. It is as if by mentioning Harry's parents or his past, or what and who he is, they would be allowing themselves to think the unthinkable. Harry is their worst nightmare – the living evidence of a terrible family secret. And he's living right there in their home.

When you compare that picture with the reality of the kind of boy Harry is, the Dursleys seem terribly sad people. Ironically, their stupidity and cruelty have prevented them from having a normal home life. True, they dote on Dudley. But only to keep him quiet and content – and that never lasts for long. Harry, as we discover, isn't an angel. Like any boy, he can misbehave and disobey, but he is great fun, and the Dursleys miss out completely on that side of his character. Harry, for his part, comes to expect their mistreatment. It is only after his first year at Hogwarts School of Witchcraft and Wizardry, when he has made good friends and enjoyed being one of the crowd, that he realises how miserable he has been with the Dursleys. That first summer holiday back at Privet Drive must have been dreadful, now that he knew how enjoyable and exciting life could be. Because he didn't realise that his mail was being intercepted by his uncle and aunt, he also thought his new friends had forgotten all about him. Knowing what he was missing must have made life even worse.

*He missed Hogwarts so much it was like having a constant stomach ache.*

Of course, the Dursleys aren't the only people who are scared of Harry and his powers. We don't yet know exactly how Harry survived the attack which killed his parents, but survive it he did, marked with the distinctive lightning-shaped scar on his forehead. His would-be murderer is left weakened and angry – the worst kind of enemy to have. Even Albus Dumbledore, the wisest wizard of them all, doesn't fully understand. When Professor McGonagall asks him about the shocking death of Harry's parents, Lily and James, he can find no explanation.

> *'They're saying he [Voldemort] tried to kill the Potters' son, Harry. But – he couldn't. He couldn't kill that little boy. No one knows why or how, but they're saying that when he couldn't kill Harry Potter, Voldemort's power somehow broke – and that's why he's gone.'*
>
> *Dumbledore nodded glumly.*
>
> *'It's – it's true?' faltered Professor McGonagall. 'After all he's done . . . all the people he's killed . . . he couldn't kill a little boy? It's just astounding . . . of all the things*

*to stop him . . . but how in the name of*
*heaven did Harry survive?'*

   *'We can only guess,' said Dumbledore, 'we*
*may never know.' . . .*

Harry's story is a very sad one. He has lost his parents and is utterly unloved by his relatives. He hasn't experienced much kindness at all in his first 11 years. Yet he is already celebrated. Just another little boy in the Muggle world, he is renowned in the world to which he was born – the magical world which exists alongside the ordinary lives of the Muggles. In that world he is Harry Potter – 'the boy who lived!'

## Darker moments

When J.K. Rowling first thought of the Harry Potter stories, she didn't see them primarily as books for children. Perhaps that's why she made no effort to simplify them. Their complications, twists and turns, red herrings, comedy, danger and extraordinary special effects only add to the excitement. The author knew from the beginning that they were going to be fun to write and that has made them fun to read too, even during the darkest, most frightening moments. Who will ever forget Harry's first encounter with a Dementor in *Harry Potter and the Prisoner of Azkaban*?

> *Its face was completely hidden beneath its hood. Harry's eyes darted downwards, and what he saw made his stomach contract. There was a hand protruding from the cloak and it was glistening, greyish, slimy-looking and scabbed, like something dead that had decayed in water . . .*

Later in the book, he discovers why his reaction to that horrible sight is so much more extreme than anybody else's.

Or what about the tense moments while Harry

sits awaiting the decision of the Sorting Hat, a 'patched, frayed and extremely dirty' pointed wizard's hat? Like every other new pupil at Hogwarts, Harry has to put the Hat on to discover which house he will be joining – Gryffindor, Hufflepuff, Ravenclaw or the dreaded Slytherin.

> *'Hmm,' said a small voice in his ear. 'Difficult. Very difficult. Plenty of courage, I see. Not a bad mind, either. There's talent, oh my goodness, yes – and a nice thirst to prove yourself, now that's interesting . . . So where shall I put you?'*

Fortunately for Harry, the Sorting Hat decides on Gryffindor, but for a moment it is touch and go, and Harry never forgets how close he came to joining Slytherin. There is definitely something that connects him to the darker side of magic. It is evident too when he finally succeeds in finding the perfect wand, an 'unusual combination –

holly and phoenix feather, eleven inches, nice and supple.' The salesman, a rather creepy gentleman, draws Harry's attention to a chilling coincidence.

> Mr Ollivander fixed Harry with his pale stare.
>
> 'I remember every wand I've ever sold, Mr Potter. Every single wand. It so happens that the phoenix whose feather is in your wand, gave another feather – just one other. It is very curious indeed that you should be destined for this wand when its brother – why its brother gave you that scar.'

It is in *Harry Potter and the Goblet of Fire* that the significance of that observation becomes terrifyingly evident in an episode during which Harry comes face to face with his nemesis, 'whiter than a skull, with wide livid scarlet eyes, and a nose that was as flat as a snake's, with slits for nostrils . . .'

# Harry's friends and other characters

The friendship between Harry, Ron and Hermione is very important in the Harry Potter books. The two boys are not especially charitable towards Hermione to begin with, thinking her pushy and over-enthusiastic about the academic side of life at Hogwarts. But eventually they realise that she is well worth including in their adventures, not least because she is very brave, as well as brainy. The three of them may have magic powers, but their friendship is very much like any other friendship between young people. They bicker and tease, but ultimately they know they can count on each other. After a particularly riveting lesson in which some of the pupils learned to confront their worst fear by making a Boggart take its shape and then laughing at it, Hermione declared her approval for the teacher, and the subject.

*'But I wish I could have had a turn with the*

*Boggart —'*

*'What would it have been for you?' said Ron, sniggering. 'A piece of homework that only got nine out of ten?'*

The teachers at Hogwarts are all fascinating individuals. They know that Harry Potter is special, but they react in very different ways. Albus Dumbledore and Professor McGonagall, the headmaster and deputy headmistress, do their best to treat him fairly, sometimes even sparing him punishments because they believe that he has acted with the best of intentions, if not always wisely. Snape, on the other hand, loathes Harry and does his best to cause him harm and undermine his popularity. Sometimes it is hard to know exactly where some of the teachers stand in relation to the extraordinary young wizard in their midst. Professor Lupin, a teacher of Defence Against the Dark Arts, begins as a mysterious character, sound asleep on the Hogwarts train.

There are no clues as to whether he will be a good or bad influence on the lives of Harry and his friends. As the story unfolds and the author begins to shed light on his character, we learn that he is far from straightforward, and that he has his own battles to fight.

The vast, dishevelled Hagrid, expelled from Hogwarts in his youth for misuse of his magic powers, is an important ally for Harry. He might not be the brightest of friends, but he is tremendously loyal in return for the loyalty that Harry, Ron and Hermione show him, often in the face of compelling evidence of his guilt.

Hagrid is also a great source of comedy. Apart from his fondness for inappropriate pets and an occasional over-indulgence in alcohol – heartily disapproved of by Hermione – he has his own dialect. It is never more distinctive than when he is excited, as he is when he discovers that the Dursleys have never told Harry about his parents, and about how they died. He realises that he is going to have to break the terrible news to their son by himself.

> *'It begins, I suppose, with – with a person called – but it's incredible yeh don't know his name, everyone in our world knows –'*
>
> *'Who?'*
>
> *'Well – I don' like sayin' the name if I can help it. No one does.'*
>
> *'Why not?'*
>
> *'Gulpin' gargoyles Harry, people are still scared. Blimey, this is difficult. See, there was this wizard who went . . . bad. As bad as you could go. Worse. Worse than worse. His name was . . . '*

Then there is Dobby, the endlessly self-reproaching house-elf who tries his best to dissuade Harry from returning to Hogwarts for the start of his second year, always speaking of himself in the third person, and of Harry – *to*

Harry – by his full name.

> *'Ah, sir,' he gasped, dabbing his face with a corner of the grubby pillow case he was wearing. 'Harry Potter is valiant and bold! He has braved so many dangers already! But Dobby has come to protect Harry Potter, to warn him, even if he does have to shut his ears in the oven doors later . . . Harry Potter must not go back to Hogwarts!'*

The scale of the cast of characters controlled by J.K. Rowling is most impressive, and the success of the books proves that children can and do revel in complex plots and settings as long as they are gripped by the story. They love a challenge. Bloomsbury, the publishers of the Harry Potter books in the UK, produced special editions of the books for adult readers because they recognised that they were being widely read by parents of young readers keen to find out what the fuss was about. Perhaps surprised to find a so-called 'children's book' so absorbing, they then recommended them to their friends. There is no difference in the story, however, only to the look of the book – the image on the jacket and the blurbs on the back cover.

## Magic games and magic books

Perhaps it is because J.K. Rowling disliked hockey so intensely at school that she invented the exhilarating game of Quidditch, which plays such a crucial part in every Harry Potter book so far. Harry is an unlikely sporting hero – he is quite small and wears glasses – but his quick thinking and nimbleness, combined with the magical powers of his Quidditch broom, make him Gryffindor's secret weapon in the endless quest to win house points. Every Quidditch match has an additional element – other scores to settle – so that there is always more at stake than the match score at the end.

J.K. Rowling's passion for books and reading is also evident in the range of fascinating titles which make their appearance in her books. Hagrid sends Harry a biting book which is only brought under control by closing it forcibly with a belt. Tom Riddle's magic diary plays a crucial part in the mystery at the heart of *Harry Potter and the Chamber of Secrets*. The reading list for all new Hogwarts pupils includes such intriguing titles as *Magical Theory* by Adalbert Waffling and *Magical Drafts and Potions* by Arsenius Jigger. And then of course there is that shameless self-publicist and bestselling author Gilderoy Lockhart – responsible for such deathless prose as *Gadding with Ghouls* and *Travelling with Trolls*, amongst others, not forgetting his autobiography, the unsurprisingly titled *Magical Me*. It is only when his incompetence is rumbled by Harry and Ron that the truth about his authorship is revealed.

*'So you've just been taking credit for what a*

*load of other people have done?' said Harry incredulously.*

*'Harry, Harry,' said Lockhart shaking his head impatiently, 'it's not nearly as simple as that. There was work involved. I had to track these people down. Ask them exactly how they managed to do what they did. Then I had to put a Memory Charm on them so they wouldn't remember doing it. If there's one thing I pride myself on, it's my Memory Charms . . .'*

Moments later, he succeeds in disarming Lockhart before he can impose one of his Memory Charms with the quick-thinking use of a spell taught to him by Snape. Lockhart lands in a crumpled heap on the floor, his reputation in ruins.

## Eager readers

There rests with J.K. Rowling a heavy

responsibility to keep her readers regularly supplied with up-to-date Harry Potter books. It is worth reminding ourselves of the literary feat she has achieved, and the challenge she has set herself for the future, all the more daunting because of the standards she has established in her first books. It is always hard, as a reader, to wait patiently for the next in a compelling series, but if we must wait, we can always re-read the previous books knowing that there is so much in them to enjoy. After J.K. Rowling's appearance at the Edinburgh International Book Festival in 1999, many of the Harry Potter books she was being asked to sign were almost worn out with re-reading and the questions asked by members of the audience showed an astonishing and impressive knowledge of the books. She was subjected to an in-depth interrogation by her readers – something she clearly loves.

But as the pompous Lockhart says, with rather less justification than his creator, 'It's not all book signings and publicity photos, you know. You want fame, you have to be prepared for a long, hard slog.'

Lindsey Fraser

May 2000

Illustrations of The Sorting Hat and Fawkes by J.K. Rowling.

# Bibliography

In date order

## Harry Potter and the Philosopher's Stone

*Bloomsbury 1997*

Harry Potter thinks he is an ordinary boy – until he is rescued by a beetle-eyed giant of a man, enrols at Hogwarts School of Witchcraft and Wizardry, learns to play Quidditch and does battle in a deadly duel. The reason: HARRY POTTER IS A WIZARD!

*Winner of the Smarties Book Prize Gold Award 1997, the British Book Awards Children's Book of the Year 1998, FCBG Children's Book Awards overall winner 1998, Young Telegraph Paperback of the Year Award 1998, Birmingham Cable Children's Book Award, Sheffield Children's Book*

*Award, The Booksellers Association/The Bookseller Author of the Year 1998, American Booksellers Book Award 1999, the Children's Book Prize 1999 of the 'Jury of Young Readers' Vienna, Kinderboekwinkel-prijs 1999, Permio Cento per la Letteratura Infantile 1998, Anne Spencer Libergh Prize in Children's Literature 1997–1998, Prix Sorcière 1999, Prix Tam-Tam 'Je bouquine' 1999, School Library Journal Best Book of the Year, American Library Association Notable Book and Best Book for Young Adults 1998, Publishers Weekly Best Book of the Year, New York Public Library Best Book of the Year, Parenting Magazine Book of the Year Award 1998, Smithsonian Notable Books for Children, Borders Books Choice for 1999, Booklist Editors' Choice 1998; shortlisted for the Carnegie Medal (commended) 1998, the Guardian Fiction Prize 1998, Deutscher Jugendliteraturpreis 1999*

## Harry Potter and the Chamber of Secrets

*Bloomsbury 1998*

Harry Potter, the wizard, is in his second year at Hogwarts School of Witchcraft and Wizardry. Little does he know that this year will be just as eventful as the last . . .

*Winner of the Smarties Book Prize Gold Award 1998, the British Book Awards Children's Book of the Year 1999, FCBG Children's Book Awards 1999, Scottish Arts Council Children's Book Award 1999, North East Book Award, North East Scotland Book Award, American Library Association Notable Book and Best Book for Young Adults 1999, Booklist Editors' Choice 1999, School Library Journal Best Book of the Year 1999; shortlisted for the Whitbread Children's Book of the Year Award 1999, the Sheffield Children's Book Award, the Guardian Fiction Prize 1999*

## Harry Potter and the Prisoner of Azkaban

*Bloomsbury 1999*

Harry Potter, along with his best friends, Ron and Hermione, is about to start his third year at Hogwarts School of Witchcraft and Wizardry. He can't wait to get back to school after the summer holidays. (Who wouldn't if they lived with the horrible Dursleys?) But when Harry gets to Hogwarts, the atmosphere is tense. There's an escaped mass murderer on the loose, and the sinister prison guards of Azkaban have been called in to guard the school . . .

*Winner of the Whitbread Children's Book of the Year Award 2000, the British Book Awards Children's Author of the Year 2000, the Smarties Book Prize Gold Award 1999, American Library Association Notable Book and Best Book for Young Adults 2000, Los Angeles Times Best Book 1999, Booklist Editors' Choice 2000; shortlisted for the Carnegie Medal*

## Harry Potter and the Goblet of Fire

*Bloomsbury 2000*

The Quidditch World Cup is the thrilling high point of Harry's summer holiday prior to his return to Hogwarts for a fourth year. There his name is drawn from the Goblet of Fire to represent Hogwarts in the Triwizard Tournament featuring Quidditch teams from Europe's greatest wizarding schools. Nervous as he is, Harry soon discovers that this is the least of his worries.

## Fantastic Beasts and where to find them

*by Newt Salamander*

## Quidditch Through the Ages

*by Kennilworthy Whisp*

Both Bloomsbury 2001

J.K. Rowling has said that she may write a companion to the Harry Potter series of books and these two hilarious volumes – spoof school textbooks – show just how entertaining such a book could be. Everybody involved in this project – J.K. Rowling, her editor, her agent and her publisher, the distributers and booksellers and many, many more – gave their time and efforts free of charge. The proceeds from the two books go to Comic Relief projects internationally, including those supporting young people in the world's poorest countries.

# Other authors in the series

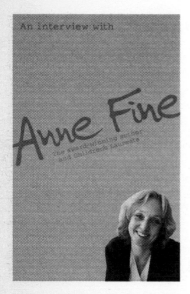

An interview with

*Anne Fine*

The award-winning author
and Children's Laureate

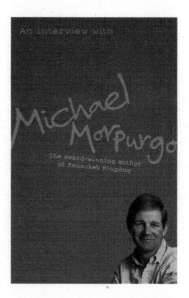

An interview with

*Michael Morpurgo*

The award-winning author
of Kensuke's Kingdom

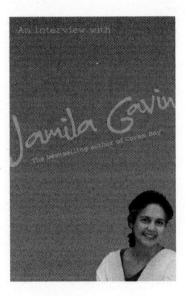

An interview with

*Jamila Gavin*

The bestselling author of Coram Boy

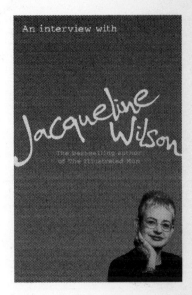

An interview with

*Jacqueline Wilson*

The bestselling author of The Illustrated Mum